*Quick Trips Series*

# Table of Contents

# Calgary

Calgary is beautifully situated in the Great Plains with the impressive Canadian Rockies looming in the distance. Calgary is the closest major city to Banff National Park and Lake Louise. It lies 185 miles south of Edmonton and 600 miles northeast of Vancouver.

More than just a tourist destination, Calgary has a rich history and leads Canada in several achievements including the major oil boom that contributed to the city's population increase. The city provides a unique combination of outdoor activities as well as arts, culture, dining, music and shopping located in the downtown neighborhoods. Calgary is the closest major city to Banff National Park and Lake Louise. It lies 185 miles south of Edmonton and 600 miles northeast of Vancouver.

The Calgary Stampede invades downtown once a year for ten days and is one of the biggest festivals in the country. Winter sports like skiing and snowboarding are extremely popular due to the Olympic-grade facilities. Fly-fishing (on the Bow and Elbow Rivers) and golfing are popular during Calgary's short yet pleasant summer.

Calgary first served as a post for the North-West Mounted Police in the late-19th century. Later the Canadian Pacific Railway allowed Calgary to grow when the town served as an important hub for the transportation of commercial goods as well as agriculture. In the 1940s, oil took over the region and the boom escalated both the population and size of the city, including a large influx of skyscrapers. Evidence of Calgary's history is displayed in museums such as the Glenbow Museum and in the Heritage Historical District.

Numerous shopping and dining options are scattered around downtown, including the popular Eau Claire Park. The local arts and music scene can be seen at small halls and galleries, including the Art Gallery of Calgary. Sports are celebrated with the Canada Sports Hall of Fame located in the Olympic Park. The effect of the 20th century oil boom is witnessed through the modern skyscrapers represented first and foremost by the popular tourist attraction – the Calgary Tower.

## Customs & Culture

Calgary houses over one million residents and is a leader in the gas and oil industries which has enabled the local economy to thrive. The city witnessed a major growth in population in the early 2000s when Calgary grew by 12.4 percent.

It's not exactly New York City; however Calgary is considered one of the 'melting pots' of Canada, third behind Toronto and Vancouver for 'visible minorities'. During the early 2000 population boom, 78 percent of Calgary's new residents were minorities with Chinese and South Asian ethnicities growing rapidly.

Calgary first thrived as a frontier paradise with cowboys, fur traders and Native Americans all converging yet it was the oil boom which really gave Calgary an identity and shortly later, a large population. Today the culture of Calgary is a combination of modern progressive industries (such as the 'Green Industry) and outdoor attractions.

The Southern Alberta Jubilee Auditorium has hosted hundreds of Broadway musicals. The Chinese Cultural Centre and Glenbow Museum are among the top destinations in the city. The city also hosted the 1988 Winter Olympics, the first in Canada and is home to the Calgary Flames of the NHL.

# Geography

The city of Calgary is located in the province of Alberta, Canada with the Bow River running through it and the scenic Canadian Rocky Mountains to its west. Calgary is finely situated with premier outdoor activities such as skiing and hiking just minutes away as well as benefiting from the nearby Banff National Park.

Calgary has a large metropolitan area divided into five neighborhoods. The busy Calgary International Airport (YYC) is the primary transportation hub for central and western Canada along with Calgary/Springbank Airport.

Transportation is provided via city buses and the light rail, known as the C-Train, and one of the first such systems in North America. The Peace Bridge along with nearly 400 other miles of path systems connects walking and bicycle traffic. Calgary's street network includes avenues and streets which are both numbered. Freeways and expressways also cross the city.

# Weather & Best Time to Visit

Calgary, like most of southwestern Canada, experiences a long, cold winter and short, moderately warm summers. The short summers see an average high of 75 degrees Fahrenheit in July with evenings that drop rapidly to 46 degrees or lower. Late-May to early-September is Calgary's 'busy season' due to the warmer temperatures.

A city of temperature extremes, Calgary winters can be unpredictable however due to the dry climate residents are faced with more cold temperatures then heavy snowfall. It is not uncommon for below-0 temperatures in the middle of the winter though with an average of 2,400+

hours of sunshine each year, Calgary remains one of Canada's sunniest cities.

While Calgary is considered a 'dry climate' keep in mind that due to the Canadian Rockies in the near distant west, weather can be unpredictable with shifts in temperature, with snowstorms in the winter and thunderstorms in the spring and summer.

# Sights & Activities: What to See & Do

## Banff National Park

224 Banff Avenue (Visitor Centre)

Banff, AB, Canada

(403) 762-1551

www.pc.gc.ca/pn-np/ab/banff/index.aspx

Calgary is the closest major city to Banff National Park,

Canada's oldest national park. The massive 2,500+ square mile park offers some of the more scenic photo opportunities in the country including the popular Lake Louise.

The Canadian Pacific Railway contributed to the early popularity of Banff when the Banff Springs Hotel and Chateau Lake Louise were constructed, followed by Great Depression-era public works projects which brought a road system to the park.

Today Banff is the most visited national park in Alberta, Canada and one of the most visited parks in North America with nearly 4 million visitors reported in the mid-2000s. Along with the majestic scenery, Banff National Park is home to more than 50 species including rare glimpses at Grizzly and black bears, wolverines, cougars, moose and wolves. Elk are common at higher elevations as are a combination of mule and white-tailed deer in the valleys. Bighorn sheep and mountain goats are also widespread.

The town of Banff is the central commercial spot in the park with famous landmarks like Cave and Basin National Historic Site, Banff Centre, Whyte Museum and Buffalo Nations Luxton Museum. If visiting make sure you spend time at the world famous Banff Upper Hot Springs.

Skiing and golfing are popular inside the park thanks to the resorts Lake Louise Mountain Resort, Sunshine Village and Mount Norquay. The 27-hole Fairmont Banff Springs Hotel golf course is world renowned.

Hiking is popular with favorite day hikes including the Cory Pass Loop, Johnson Lake, Fenland Trail, Silverton Falls, Bow River, C-Level Cirque, Tunnel Mountain and Sulphur Mountain. Backcountry hiking and camping is accessible with a permit along with traditional camping. Difficult trails (which will enable you to beat some of the crowds) can be found at: Harvey Pass, Aylmer Lookout and Aylmer Pass.

Banff National Park connects to other national forest including Jasper National Park (to the north), Yoho National Park (to the west) and Kootenay National Park (to the south). A park pass is required to see the sights; however if you plan to simply drive through the park (via the Trans-Canada Highway) admittance is free.

# Lake Louise

224 Banff Avenue

Banff, AB, Canada

(403) 762-8421

www.skilouise.com

Lake Louise is one of the most popular attractions inside Banff National Park. The hamlet was named after Princess Louise Caroline Alberta, the fourth daughter of Queen Victoria, and is divided into two separate communities: The Village and Lake Louise Mountain Resort.

The Village is adjacent to the Trans-Canada Highway and provides a visitor center, mall, deli, grill and bar. The more popular Lake Louise Mountain Resort ski area is located across the highway and at a higher elevation, next to the notorious emerald lake.

Chateau Lake Louise is the famous landmark at the ski resort which is a good day-trip for those who cannot afford to stay at the luxurious hotel over night. Skiing is the most popular activity at Lake Louise though the nearby Moraine Lake provides the iconic shot of the Valley of the Ten Peaks which was pictured on the back of the $20 Canadian banknote from 1969 to 1979.

If you want to get out and truly enjoy nature at its finest consider camping during Lake Louise's short yet incredible summer season. Popular campgrounds include: Johnston Canyon Campground, Mosquito Creek Campground, Protection Mountain Campground and Tunnel Mountain. Less popular yet outstanding campgrounds include: Castle Mountain, Lake Louise (tent only) and Two Jack Main Campground.

Saddleback Pass, Fairview Mountain, Mirror Lake, Devil's Thumb, Mount Whyte, Lake Agnes and other mountainous sights are accessible via hiking trails in the area. Mountain biking, horseback riding, kayaking, fishing, canoeing and rafting are popular activities during the summer while the aforementioned alpine skiing, snowboarding, cross-country skiing and ice fishing dominate the winter.

# Calgary Tower

9th Ave and Centre St. SW

Calgary, AB, Canada

403-266-7171

www.calgarytower.com

The Calgary Tower just might get lost in the abundance of skyscrapers now present in downtown. It was once the tallest skyscraper in the city limits (626 ft) and it is a popular tourist attraction. In just over one minute you can reach the top courtesy of an elevator which offers some of the best views of the city, mountains and prairies.

The rotating restaurant will interest the children while you indulge in a drink or two at the cocktail lounge.* Education programs for young children are now available and a new art gallery has recently been opened inside the tower as well.

If you're looking to bring back some gifts for family or friends Calgary Tower has a shop with your typical tourist collectibles and clothing.

The elevator ride is $12.95 for adults, $10.95 for seniors, $9.95 for youth and $5.00 for children. Children 3 and under get in free. The Calgary Tower is open every day of the year aside from Christmas Day. July and August the tower is open until 10pm while the rest of the year the hours are 9am to 9pm.

*Note that the restaurant only does a complete rotation at noon.

## Fort Calgary Historic Park

750 9th Avenue SE

Calgary, AB, Canada

(403) 268-8500

www.heritagepark.ca

The biggest historical village in the country, Fort Calgary Historic Park takes you back to the early 19th century as you literally walk through the time period which built Calgary from the ground up.

More than just the iconic fort which was placed on Calgary to regulate trade in the area, the historic park also features horse-drawn carriages, grain mills, steam engines, paddlewheels, vintage churches and schools. Enjoy street theater including costumed actors who play the roles of former citizens of Calgary from 1860 through 1915.

The original train station (built in 1890) at Lake Louise is preserved and featured now at Heritage Park. Located next to Glenmore Reservoir, visitors may also ride on the water courtesy of the paddlewheel which will certainly be one of your children's favorite memories of the entire vacation.

Educational programs and private events are also hosted at Fort Calgary Historic Park. For more information on these seasonal events, visit http://www.heritagepark.ca to discover what is taking place during your stay.

Fort Calgary Historic Park is open year-round every day (excluding a few holidays) from 9am to 5pm. Admission is $15 for adults and $10 for children.

# Calgary Zoo & Botanical Gardens

1300 Zoo Road NE

Calgary, AB, Canada, T2E 7V6

(403) 232-9300

Nearly 1,000 animals live inside Calgary Zoo where the park has been thoughtfully designed to provide the most natural habitats possible for its year-round residents. In the summer gorgeous natural flora and fauna of the region is on display and in the winter visitors will enjoy the year-round tropical butterfly enclosure.

The notoriously popular exhibits inside the zoo are the African lions, woodland caribou, whooping cranes, penguins, hippos, giraffes, cougars and bears. Dining, souvenirs, rides, play areas and other guest services are available inside the park.

It is very easy to spend a half to full day inside the massive zoo and botanical gardens; however if you still have time and energy try to allow for a visit inside the

Prehistoric Park which adjoins the zoo. Here you will walk back to the past, the Prehistoric era to be exact, where children will relish in the opportunity to interact with extinct dinosaurs and other creatures.

The Calgary Zoo & Botanical Gardens are open 10am-5pm, $10 for adults and $10 for children. Children two and younger attend free. Also note that parking is $7.

## Telus Spark (World of Science Museum)

220 St. Georges Drive NE

Calgary, AB, Canada, AB 2TE 5T2

(403) 221-3700

www.calgaryscience.ca

The family-oriented Telus Spark World of Science

Museum in Calgary is an interactive journey through outer space including a planetarium (footage in high-definition) and other exhibits.

One of the highlights of Telus Spark is Lego Mindstorms, an exhibit where children can build a functioning robot from scratch out of Legos. There are also a number of other interactive programs to keep your family entertained. Traveling exhibitions are also hosted at Telus Spark as well as events, including an Adult's Only night.

And, while in the area, it is highly recommended you stop next door by Shaw Millennium Park which is one of the largest skateboard parks in North America with 75,000 square feet of playground cement as well as basketball and volleyball courts.

Shaw Millennium Park is open to the general public while Telus Spark World of Science Museum is open 9am to 5pm. Admission is $20 (adults), $15 (youth), $13 (children) and children 3 and under are free. It is also $5 to park at Telus Spark World of Science Museum.

# Eau Claire Market & Prince's Island Park

2nd Ave. SW & 3rd St. SW

Calgary, AB, Canada

(403) 264-6450

www.eauclairemarket.com

www.calgary.ca/CSPS/Parks/Pages/Locations/Downtown-parks/Princes-Island-Park.aspx

Escape downtown traffic in the car-free Eau Claire Market for a lovely afternoon of shopping and dining. The busy

Eau Claire Market features the premier restaurants, bars, shops and other activities in Calgary if you are searching for the ‘hot spot’.

Additional entertainment options inside the market include a cinema and IMAX theater, and if that is not enough you’ll need to allow time to visit Prince’s Island Park* which connects directly to Eau Claire Market.

The island is one of the top places in all of Calgary to spend a beautiful afternoon as you meander through a path system which follows the Bow River and offers unique glimpses at one of the country’s most famous species – Canadian geese. Also, if you travel during the summer make sure you look into the entertainment lineup at the outdoor grass amphitheater.

Additional features of Prince's Island Park include: picnic areas, playground, canoeing along the Bow River, flower gardens, the ChevronTexaco Learning Pathway and water fountains. During the winter outdoor skating is available on the lagoon along with opportunities to cross-country ski.

Parking is available underneath and around Eau Claire Market. The evening and weekend rates begin at 5pm with the flat rate at $2. It is recommended to visit the market by foot if you are staying nearby and/or can take public transit.

The restaurants and shops located at Eau Claire Market have varying hours yet best advice is to visit late-morning to early-afternoon.

*NOTE: Prince's Island Park, like other landmarks around Calgary experienced flood damage during the summer of 2013. Work crews are currently working to restore popular sightseeing attractions like Prince's Island Park which will hopefully be fully restored in the next year or two.

## Scotiabank Saddledome (Home of Calgary Flames)

555 Saddledome Rise SE

Calgary, AB, Canada, T2G 2W1

(403) 777-4646

www.scotiabanksaddledome.com

Like a lot of major cities in Canada, hockey is a "religion". The Scotiabank Saddledome, home to the Calgary Flames, features 41 regular season games if you are visiting between October and April.

The 19,000+ arena is also home to the Calgary Hitmen of the Western Hockey League and Calgary Roughnecks of the National Lacrosse League. The venue also hosts concerts and if you are attending the Calgary Exhibition and Stampede in July, you'll likely spend a lot of time inside the arena as it's one of the primary venues for the festival.

Tickets for the Calgary Flames start at $40 for the 2013-14 NHL season and go up to nearly $270 for seats by the ice. The Flames usually sell out home games so if you want to take in one of Canada's strongest traditions it is recommended you purchase tickets in advance of the event.

For a complete list of upcoming events (as well as tickets) visit: www.scotiabanksaddledome.com

## Calgary Exhibition & Stampede

1410 Olympic Way SE

Calgary, AB, Canada

(403) 261-0101

Or 1-800-661-1260

www.calgarystampede.com

Early-July is the most crowded time for Calgary as the city is invaded by the annual rodeo, exhibition and festival with many tourists visiting from out of town. The ten-day event is one of the largest festivals in all of Canada and is billed 'The Greatest Outdoor Show on Earth'.

The Calgary Exhibition and Stampede dates back to 1886 when Calgary held its first fair and today the annual gathering continues to celebrate the city's past with a parade, stage shows, massive rodeo, agricultural competitions, chuckwagon racing and concerts.

The Stampede generally draws some of the biggest names in country and rock music – past and present. In 2013, Hedley, Dixie Chicks, Tim McGraw and Kiss highlighted a bill which featured more than 50 bands.

The Rangeland Derby is also highly unique to the stampede and one of the events you'll want to make sure to visit. Dating back to the 1920s, the 'half-mile of hell' chuckwagon race features 30+ teams all competing for over a million dollars in prizes.

Visitors with interest in Native American culture will also appreciate that five tribes are well represented at the 'Indian Village' near the Elbow River on the southern section of the Calgary Stampede. In fact, individuals of the First Nations were highly involved in the first official Stampede of 1912 and continue to be an integral part of the festival.

Calgary is also radically transformed during this time period as office buildings and shops are decorated in themes to match residents and tourists who wear cowboy and other Western gear from the early 20th century. The aroma alone from the numerous barbecues in the area will be enough to stimulate the senses.

If you are traveling to Calgary during early-July the Calgary Exhibition and Stampede is a must-see but bar in mind that available lodging is increasingly difficult to find during this time period so be sure to book early. Also, expect difficulties navigating around town as traffic will surely be increased.

Tickets to the Calgary Stampede depend on what you want to witness. High-profile concerts are sold on an individual basis as are tickets to the rodeo and chuckwagon race. Other concerts, shopping opportunities and food vendors are open to the general public.

## Canada Olympic Park & Plaza

88 Canada Olympic Road SW

Calgary, AB, Canada

(403) 247-5452

www.winsportcanada.ca

In 1988, Calgary made history by being the first city in the country to host the Winter Olympics. Now more than twenty years in the past, Canada Olympic Park/Plaza remembers Calgary's role in the world's greatest winter sports celebration.

Olympic Park was the site for ski jumping, luge and bobsledding during the 1988 Games and remains world-class facilities. The Scotiabank Saddledome (home to the Calgary Flames) was also built to provide a venue for figure skating and hockey during the competition.

Today the plaza houses the Olympic Hall of Fame and Museum – the world's largest collection of Olympic artifacts – as well as in-depth coverage of local athletes from Canada.

The museum is outstanding but what really makes the park enjoyable is the opportunity to look and feel like an Olympic athlete as downhill and cross-country ski lessons, snowboard lessons, skating and ski jumping are all available during the winter along with luge and bobsled rides. In the summer, partake in the mountain-bike course or take the chairlift up to the ski-jump tower for photo opportunities.

The Canada Olympic Park is connected closely with WinSport (Winter Sport Institute) which is instrumental in providing community activities, namely youth sports like hockey, skiing, snowboarding and skating. Zip lining and a climbing wall are also available at the park during the summer.

Daily tours of Canada Olympic Park are available from 10am to 4pm. The hours of the ski hill vary by season.

Admission and ride information is available at:

www.winsportcanada.ca

# Glenbow Museum

130 9 Ave SE

Calgary, AB, Canada

(403) 268-4100

www.glenbow.org

You can learn everything about the history of Calgary at the Glenbow Museum. Located downtown in the hear of Calgary's Cultural District (across from the Calgary Tower), the Glenbow Museum takes you through the history of Alberta (including extensive coverage of local

Native American tribes) and concludes with the local oil boom which contributed much of Calgary's expansion in the 20th century.

The museum, art gallery, library and archives combine to present over a million artifacts with some 28,000 works of art making it one of the biggest collections in all of Canada.

There is a permanent collection at Glenbow as well as rotating exhibitions from outside sources. History is not the only subject presented as there is also a great deal of art. According to the museum's official statement, "the museum builds on a commitment to preserve our cultural and western heritage while simulataneously providing visitors with a glimpse of the world beyond'.

The Glenbow Museum charges $14 for adults, $10 for seniors, $9 for students and youth. The 'Family Rate', which might be your best deal, gets admission to the museum for two adults and four children at $32. Also, children six and under get in free.

## Stephen Avenue Walk

8th Avenue SW between 4th Street SW & 1 Street SE

Calgary, AB, Canada

(403) 215-1570

www.calgarydowntown.com/saw.html

Along with Eau Claire Market, Stephen Avenue Walk is the most popular pedestrian mall/market in Calgary. The walk offers an abundance of restaurants, cafes, pubs and bars as well as high-end retail boutiques and department stores.

During the peak summer hours it is not uncommon to walk past thousands of people who embark on Stephen Avenue to take in live performances, artist stands, portable vendors and cultural stands.

It's a shopping paradise with nine major shopping centers or department stores along with highly rated cafes, restaurants and pubs. While exploring the region make sure you check out the Walk of Fame which profiles 55 celebrities that were either born in Calgary of left a major impression on the city.

Stephen Avenue is also home to the Telus Convention Centre and houses some of the more famous historical buildings in the city; the majority of them designed in sandstone which was the norm after a devastating fire in 1886 which damaged several Calgary establishments.

Looking for a night spot? Stephen Avenue Walk isn't nearly as popular as 17 Avenue at night, although there are a few pubs to visit after dark. Unlike Eau Claire Market, Stephen Avenue Walk is also open to automobiles from 6am to 6pm.

## Chinatown (Chinese Cultural Centre)

197 1 Street SW

Calgary, AB, Canada, AB T2P 4M4

(403) 262-5071

www.culturalcentre.ca

Connoisseurs of Chinese culture should make Chinatown

one of their must-see sights while visiting Calgary. Your first stop should be the impressive Chinese Cultural Centre.

Constructed in 1993, the Chinese Cultural Centre features a spectacular 70 foot dome painted with over 500 dragons and other imagery symbolic to Chinese culture. The centre was inspired by Beijing's Temple of Heaven and celebrates the rich Chinese culture located inside Calgary.

The construction of the $10 million facility was completed in 1992 and since then the cultural center has been the focal point for the rich Chinese culture evident both in Calgary and the surrounding region.

During your stay make sure you walk through the rotating art and cultural exhibitions with a museum which houses sacred Chinese artifacts. There are also courses available related to martial arts, sports, leisure and languages.

The Chinese Cultural Centre is open 9am to 9pm daily. Entrance is free though donations are kindly accepted.

## Art Gallery of Calgary

117 8 Avenue SW

Calgary, AB, Canada

(403) 770-1350

www.artgallerycalgary.org

The small yet intimate Art Gallery of Calgary is one of the best options to experience art and culture in downtown Calgary outside the Glenbow Museum.

Located at Stephen Avenue Mall which also offers its fair share of shopping and dining options, the Art Gallery of Calgary provides a contemporary art gallery which features exhibits from local, national and international artists.

After you wander through the historic building treat yourself to a cup of coffee or tea on the sidewalk patio. It's a prime spot for people watching and there is always some form of culture in Calgary to embrace.

The Art Gallery of Calgary is open Tuesday-Saturday 10am to 5pm. Admission is $5 for adults, $2.50 for students and children 6 and under are free.

# Budget Tips

##  Accommodation

### Sandman Inn

888 7th Ave SW (Downtown Branch), Calgary, AB,

Canada,

(403) 237-8626 or 1-800-SANDMAN

www.sandmanhotels.ca/calgary

The Sandman Inn is a series of budget-friendly motels.

They are scattered throughout the city including one location next to the Calgary Airport and another downtown by the city centre.

Rooms begin at $79, and the downtown branch – you're best bet if you plan to stay for more than a few days – is not far from 17th Avenue (Calgary's retail district), Scotiabank Saddledome, Telus Convention Centre, Stampede Park and more.

The City Centre branch features an indoor pool, whirlpool, Moxie's Grill & Bar and Mbar Lounge.

## Canada's Best Value Inn

2416 16th Avenue NW

Calgary, AB, Canada

Canada's Best Value Inn is an alternative to the Calgary Motel Village which provides more than 20 motel chains and is one of the central spots for guests visiting the city of Calgary. The village is dominated by nationwide chains such as Super 8, Ramada, Best Western and Day's Inn therefore the top options for budget rooms.

However, if you would like to be closer to downtown Canada's Best Value Inn is a pleasant alternative. The hotel features a seasonal outdoor pool and free Wi-Fi in every room. Other amenities include a microwave and refrigerator, cable TV and continental breakfast.

Like a lot of destinations, summer rates are higher than winter rates (excluding popular ski areas like at Lake Louise) and you'll pay more on a weekend compared to weekday. Rooms typically start at around $70 and will be higher during peak time.

# Centro Motel

4540 16th Avenue NW

Calgary, AB, Canada

(403) 288-6658

www.centromotel.com

The Centro Motel is self-defined as a ‘boutique motel’ after an old building was remolded into the current motel in 2010. As a result, Centro Motel is up-to-date with new beds and furnishing with a progressive, sophisticated feel.

The motel offers free Wi-Fi and rooms with a flat-screen TV. Other amenities include a free continental breakfast, free long distance calls, an iPod docking station in all rooms and internet café in the lobby.

Centro Motel is pet-friendly (the motel requests that guests inform of number and types of pets in reservation) and minutes away from McMahon Stadium (home of the Calgary Stampeders) as well as Foothills Athletic Park. Located just off 16th Avenue and Trans-Canada Hwy (Hwy 1), the Centro Motel is perfectly located for quick access to the rest of the city as well as travel to Banff National Park.

Rooms at the Centro Motel begin in the high-$90s and low-$100s depending on day of week and season.

# Westin Calgary

320 4 Avenue SW

Calgary, AB, Canada, T2P 2S6

(403) 266-1611

www.westincalgary.com

The thriving international commerce of Calgary has shot hotel rates through the roof as businesspeople travel to the city on a routine basis. Therefore, you can expect your traditional brands like Sheraton, Delta and Westin to provide budget to moderate rates downtown and sprinkled throughout the rest of the city.

The Westin is slightly higher than your traditional budget option yet still within most travelers' means depending on what you plan to fork over for a room. The large, 500+

central downtown location is outstanding with quality rooms starting in the mid to low $200s.

Amenities include triple sheeting and down blankets, private bathrooms, laptop-compatible safes and multi-line phones with voice mail if you are traveling for work.

## EconoLodge

2440 16th Avenue NW

Calgary, AB, T2M 0M5

(403) 289-2561

www.econolodgecalgary.com

Two locations: the EconoLodge Inn & Suites University and EconoLodge Motel Village are open to guests in Calgary. Based in northwest Calgary, both locations are conveniently located off the Trans-Canada Highway for quick access to the rest of the city as well as public transportation via the LRT (Light Rail Transit).

The EconoLodge provides a free continental breakfast, parking, wireless internet access and local calls. You should expert to pay higher rates during the Calgary Stampede where booking a room well in advance is highly recommended for travelers.

Rooms at the EconoLodge start in the high-$90s and low-$100s.

# Restaurants, Cafés & Bars

## 1886 Buffalo Café

187 Barclay Parade SW, Calgary, AB, Canada

(403) 269-9255

www.1886buffalocafe.ca

The 1886 Buffalo Café was actually founded in the year of its title and received a publicity boost during the 1988 Winter Olympics. It's your classic small-town diner which specializes in breakfast and will leave you stuffed until well after lunch. The authentic, pioneer-era décor is the best environment of any restaurant in the city representing its proud cowboy heritage.

Kenny's Special is the mountain high plate of egg, cheese, mushroom and green pepper favorite. Other dishes on the menu for breakfast range from Steak & Eggs to Ed's Benedicts, Huevos Rancheros to The Blaisey Boy Omelet. Buffalo Café is located directly across the street from Eau Claire Market.

It's a little more than your typical diner breakfast with menu items that range from $10 to $15 though well worth the cost.

## Mercato

2224 4 Street SW

Calgary, AB, Canada

(403) 263-5535

www.mercatogourmet.com

Mercato is what you would define as the ideal restaurant: ideal in the fact that its environment is top-notch but furthermore the menu matches its environment. The casual open kitchen serves delicious Italian and the dinner hour gets quite lively with an energetic atmosphere.

If you dine during the summer, request a table on the street-side patio and make sure to check out their wine selection. Menu prices are a little higher than other options yet you truly get what you pay for at Mercato.

## Blink

111 8 Avenue SW

Calgary, AB, Canada, T2P 1B4

(403) 263-5330

www.blinkcalgary.com

Locally and nationally acclaimed, Blink has only been open since 2007 yet is a constant among Top Picks for its trendy gastro located within the heart of Calgary.

Contemporary and sophisticated, you really can't go wrong with anything on the menu and you can even learn more about the culinary process through their monthly cooking classes.

Blink is located on Stephen Avenue Walk not too far from the Art Gallery of Calgary. Check out the menu, hours and learn more about the cooking classes at: www.blinkcalgary.com. Blink is closed on Sundays.

# Lido Café

144 10 Street NW

Calgary, AB, Canada

(403) 283-0131

www.lidocafe.ca

Despite gentrification taking place all around it, Lido hasn't lost anything about it roots from the 'cash-only' policy to prices which almost feel 20th century (example, a hearty meatloaf sandwich goes for $6).

The ultimate neighborhood joint from a previous decade food is available for takeout as well and the breakfast might not quite stack up to 1886 Buffalo Café yet it is darn good in its own right. If you want a burger in town and would rather bypass McDonalds, Lido Café is your spot.

## River Café

25 Prince's Island Park

Calgary, AB, Canada

(403) 261-7670

www.river-cafe.com

The name is surely enough to get most excited yet this upscale restaurant has more than just a title. Winner of critic awards for its menu, River Café has the perfect location in Calgary on Prince's Island.

The menu is constantly rotated with items selected both on available ingredients and season. And, if you are traveling during the summer, with 24 hours notice River Café will prepare a picnic hamper for you to enjoy on Prince's Island elsewhere.

River Café cooks a lot of their meals wood-fired and serve organic whole breads. Several vegetarian dishes are also available from the wide, contemporary menu.

The café is open seven days a week with hours that go well past dark. Prices on the menu vary greatly with budget-friendly options starting at $12 and stretching close to $40 per plate. Reservations are recommended.

# Shopping

## Alberta Boot

50 50 Avenue SE

Calgary, AB, Canada

(403) 263-4623

www.albertaboot.com

When you visit Calgary you'll want to make sure your credit card is nearby because the city truly is one of the retail powerhouses of North America. In fact, Calgary's economic prosperity is most appropriately represented by the number of retail centers, massive malls, boutique shops and niche stores which have rushed to the city in the past couple of decades.

However, if you don't want to forget Calgary's roots make sure you take time to visit Alberta Boot. The factory and store is the only boot manufacture in Alberta which makes it the number one shop for boots (made in a number of hides from kangaroo to python, alligator to original cowhide).

# Mountain Equipment Co-Op (MEC)

830 10th Avenue SW

Calgary, AB, Canada

(403) 269-2420

www.mec.ca

In addition to Alberta Boot, Mountain Equipment Co-Op (MEC) is the authentic regional store for all outdoor equipment. Before you visit Banff National Park or Lake

Louise make sure you have all the necessary supplies from the gigantic Co-Op store which specializes in equipment, travel gear and clothing.

# Chinook Centre

6455 Macleod Trail SW

Calgary, AB, Canada

(403) 259-2022

www.chinookcentre.com

The Chinook Centre is the place to go with the entire family as the massive mall offers over 200 retails stores, twenty-five restaurants, three major department stores and a movie theater.

If you are only going to shop at one retail center during your visit to Calgary make sure you make it the Chinook

Centre. Everything about the mall is world class, from its stylish architecture and design to the sheer abundance of retail options and other entertainment options.

## Smithbuilt Hats

1103 12th Street SE

Calgary, AB, Canada

(403) 244-9131

www.smithbuilthats.com

Modern-day Calgary might make it easy to forget about the roots of the city but it's important to remember that the region was first and foremost a hub for cowboys and Native Americans, fur traders and outdoorsmen.

Thus, it is great to see that the history of Calgary is still preserved (even in retail) thanks to manufactures like Smithbuilt Hats.

Smithbuilt Hats not only sells authentic, cowhide-made hats but also presents to its customers how they are made. The company has been making hats for over a century and tours are provided for those who would like to see the manufacturing process first-hand.

# Uptown 17

14 St. SW to 2 St. SW, Calgary, AB, Canada

(403) 245-1703

www.17thave.ca

Uptown 17 is an up-scale series of stores, restaurants, galleries and other services located south of downtown in the Mount Royal Village. It is the premiere destination for marquee boutique shops and the latest fashion trends.

Unlike other malls, like the Chinook Centre, Uptown 17 is an opportunity to walk outside on a nice summer day and take in the vibe of Calgary as well.

## Know Before You Go

#  Entry Requirements

To visit Canada as a tourist you will need a valid travel document, such as a passport, a certificate of good health and a clean record with absolutely no criminal convictions. Additionally, you may be asked to convince immigration officers of strong ties with your home country, your intent to leave at the end of your stay and your means to support yourself financially for the duration of your stay. In most cases, you will also need an entry document in the form of either a visitor visa or, in the case of citizens of countries that are visa exempt, an Electronic Travel Authorization (eTA). Visitors from the USA, members of the Royal Family and French residents of St. Pierre and Miquelon are the only persons exempt from needing an eTA. In the case of family groups, each family member will need to apply separately for an Electronic Travel Authorization. Countries exempted from requiring a visa include the United Kingdom (and British Overseas Territories such as Gibraltar, Pitcairn Island, the Falkland Islands, the Cayman Islands, Montserrat, Bermuda, the British Virgin Islands, St Helena, Anguilla, the Turks and Caicos Islands), Australia, New Zealand, Belgium, the Netherlands, France, Greece, Cyprus, Austria, Germany, Denmark, Finland, Sweden, Norway, Iceland, Spain, Portugal, Switzerland, Italy, Ireland, Hungary,

Poland, the Czech Republic, Japan, Croatia, Slovenia, Slovakia, Latvia, Lithuania, Liechtenstein, Malta, Monaco, San Marino, Andorra, Samoa, Papua New Guinea, the Solomon Islands, Chile, the Republic of Korea and Singapore. A visitor's visa is valid for 6 months and you can apply to have this extended by 30 days.

## Health insurance

Medical treatment can be expensive in Canada and the Canadian government does not offer any payment for medical treatment. There are no reciprocal agreements between Canada and the UK, the European Union or Australia regarding medical treatment. For this reason, visitors should make arrangements for sufficient health insurance to cover any medical emergencies as well as repatriation, if it is required, before leaving home. Temporary health insurance can be arranged through a Canadian agency for a period of up to 365 days, with premiums starting at between $20 and $25. When considering insurance policies, do bear in mind that some extreme outdoor sports like skiing may not be covered automatically by your policy. If you are planning to participate in activities not normally covered, you should make arrangements for additional cover.

# Travelling with Pets

When travelling with pets to Canada, the first requirement is the submission of proper travel documents. In the case of dogs, the animal will need to be inspected at the point of entry and a fee for this is levied at $30. All points of entry to Canada have an animal inspector on duty, which means that advance notification is not required.

Cats entering Canada do not need to be quarantined or microchipped, but they will need to be accompanied by a detailed rabies vaccination certificate or a health certificate stating that they are from a country recognized by Canada as rabies free. In the case of pets from the European Union, a pet passport will be accepted as alternative, provided it contains all the required details. Guide dogs and other assistance dogs are exempt from most of the restrictions that apply to other animal importations.

No import certificate is required for most reptiles and amphibians, with the exception of tortoises and turtles, in which case an application must be made a minimum of 30 days prior to import date to the Canadian Food Inspection Agency. Pet birds need to spend at least 45 days in quarantine, where a CFIA inspector will inspect their health. Application for quarantine must be made prior to your arrival in Canada. You will also need to make a declaration stating that the bird(s) have been in your possession for a minimum of 90 days and have not been in contact with other birds during that period. Birds originating from China, Vietnam, Bangladesh, Egypt, India and Indonesia are prohibited from entering Canada.

# Airports

**Toronto Pearson International Airport** (YYZ) is the busiest airport in Canada in terms of passenger traffic. Located 22.5km northwest of Toronto's downtown area, it provides access to Toronto, the capital of Ontario as well as the Golden Horseshoe, Canada's most populous region. Terminal 1, its primary terminal is one of the largest buildings of its kind in the world and its modern facilities are streamlined by the ThyssenKrupp Express Walkway, one of the fastest people-moving walkways in the world. The airport also has shops, a variety of eateries and free Wi-Fi coverage. A second airport serving Toronto is the **Billy Bishop Toronto City Airport** (YTZ), named after Canada's top flying ace from World War 1. It is located on an island in Toronto Harbour. From the airport, Toronto's CBD can be reached via a pedestrian tunnel from Eireann Quay or a scheduled ferry service. The airport falls under the Toronto Port Authority and is co-administered with the city's harbour. Besides three runways, there is also a base for seaplanes.

Ontario's third major airport is the **Ottawa/Macdonald–Cartier International Airport** (YOW), the 6th busiest in Canada and 2nd busiest in the province. It serves Ottawa, but also offers connections to the bustling centers of Toronto and Montreal as well as a gateway to the Arctic.

**Vancouver International Airport** (YVR) lies on Sea Island in Richmond, about 12km from the downtown area of Vancouver City. Although planning for the airport began as early as 1929, the site first served as a Royal Canadian Air Force base during World War Two and the proposed civilian airport only became a reality after the war. As a Pacific Gateway, Vancouver International Airport provides non-stop connections to Asia and the International Terminal offers United States Border Preclearance facilities. The multi-award-winning airport welcomes visitors to Canada with a striking collection of Aboriginal art in the form of wooden sculptures and totem poles as well as the YVR Aquarium with over 800 marine species. Regular airport personnel are backed by a team of volunteers, trained to assist travellers in navigating their way through the airport. To aid the disabled, special wheelchair lifts have been installed and check-in counters have headsets for travellers with hearing disabilities. The rapid transit Sky Train connects to Vancouver's metro rail service. Vancouver International Airport also offers free Wi-Fi coverage. The second busiest airport in British Columbia is **Victoria International Airport** (YYJ), which offers access to Vancouver Island. Recently renovated, it has various features for disabled travellers, including wheel chair friendly facilities, large signage, phones with augmented transmission and relieving areas for service dogs. The airport is set in scenic surroundings and environmental management is a high priority. Several of its ground vehicles are electrically powered and there is a bicycle assembly station just outside the main terminal as well as a bike path.

**Montréal–Pierre Elliott Trudeau International Airport** (YUL), formerly known as Montréal–Dorval International Airport, is located in the suburb of Dorval, about 20km from downtown Montreal. Utilized from the 1940s, it provides access to Montreal and Quebec, but can also serve as a gateway to parts of Ontario and even Vermont and New York in the USA. Like Vancouver, it offers United States Border Preclearance facilities, making it a modern and people friendly trans border terminal. Find your way around the airport easily with the YULi smartphone app. For easy access from the airport, a shuttle bus service connects travellers to the metro service to stops at Lionel-Groulx metro station, Central Station and Berri-UQAM metro station. **Halifax Stanfield International Airport** (YHZ) provides access to the mainland of Nova Scotia as well as its nearby maritime regions. **Winnipeg James Armstrong Richardson International Airport** (YWG) first opened in 1928 and is one of Canada's oldest airports. It is located about

10km from Winnipeg's downtown area and offers access to Winnipeg and the province of Manitoba. Additionally, it also serves as a gateway to the remote northern regions. One of its original hangars has been converted to an aviation museum, where visitors can view a collection of historical bush planes as well as Canada's first helicopter.

The province of Alberta is served by two large airports. **Calgary International Airport** (YYC) offers access to its most populous city and the majestic Canadian Rocky Mountains. First opened in 1938, it has entered a transitional phase with its new facilities scheduled for opening at the end of October 2016. If you have a few hours to while away, visit the Space Port, where you can enjoy simulated space flights or view artefacts on loan from NASA. **Edmonton International Airport** (YEG) is located about 26km from downtown Edmonton and offers a gateway to the Northern part of Alberta. Both Calgary and Edmonton have United States Border Preclearance facilities. **Kuujjuaq Airport** (YVP) is located about 2.8km southwest of Kuujjuaq in Quebec and provides access to the remote Nunavik region. It is a mandatory frequency airport, which means that it does not have sufficient air traffic to warrant a control tower.

# Airlines

Air Canada is the flag carrier and largest airline in Canada. It was founded from Trans-Canada Airlines in the 1930s, renamed in the 1960s and privatized in the 1980s, following the deregulation of Canada's air travel industry. The service flies to over 100 international and domestic destinations and is linked by codeshare agreement to 28 other international airlines, including Lufthansa, United Airlines, Aegean Airlines, EgyptAir, Jet Airways, Turkish Airlines, Singapore Airlines, Air India, Air China, All Nippon Airways and Scandinavian Airlines.

WestJet is a Canadian budget airline that was founded in the mid-1990s. Currently it is the second largest carrier in Canada, flying up to 20 million passengers annually to over 100 destinations. The airline offers no-frills service and embraces environmentally sustainable strategies. Jazz Aviation is a regional service that connects passengers to over 75 destinations in Canada and the USA. Another budget airline is Sunwing Airlines, which is based in Toronto and was recently acquired by the US tour operator, Vacation Express. Perimeter Aviation is the largest regional aircraft carrier in Manitoba and offers connections to 23 destinations in Manitoba and Ontario. It also supports the region's medical evacuation services.

Air Inuit is collectively owned by the Inuit community of Nunavik and it offers connections to domestic destinations in Quebec, Nunavut, Newfoundland and Labrador. Calm Air is a regional service that provides regional connections between the northern parts of Manitoba and Nunavut. It is based at Thompson in Manitoba. Pacific Coastal Airlines connects travellers to destinations in British Columbia. Another regional carrier serving British Columbia is the family run Orca Airways.

Toronto Pearson International Airport serves as the largest hub for Air Canada, but the airline also operates hubs at Montréal–Pierre Elliott Trudeau International Airport, where it is based, Calgary International Airport and Vancouver International Airport. Additionally, it has a strong presence at the international airports of Edmonton, Halifax, Ottawa and Winnipeg. The primary hub for the budget carrier WestJet is Toronto Pearson International Airport. Its second hub is at Calgary International Airport, where it is based. WestJet also has a strong presence at Edmonton International Airport, Vancouver International Airport and Winnipeg James Armstrong Richardson International Airport. The primary base for Jazz Airline is at Halifax Stanfield International Airport.

Jazz also has hubs at Vancouver International Airport, Calgary International Airport, Toronto Pearson International Airport and Montréal–Pierre Elliott Trudeau International Airport. Winnipeg James Armstrong Richardson International Airport and Thompson Airport serve as hubs for Perimeter Aviation. Kuujjuaq Airport is the main operating base for Inuit Air. Calm Air has two primary hubs at Thompson Airport and Winnipeg James Armstrong Richardson International Airport and secondary hubs at Churchill Airport in Manitoba and Rankin Inlet in Nunavut. Vancouver International Airport serves as the main hub for Pacific Coastal Airlines and also serves as a hub for Orca Airways.

# Money Matters

## Currency

The currency for Canada is the Canadian Dollar, which is often fairly close in value to the US dollar. The currency is available in denominations of $5, $10, $20, $50, and $100. Coins are issued in denominations of 5c (a nickel), 10c (a dime), 25c (a quarter), $1 (a loonie) and $2 (a toonie or twoonie). In 2011, Canada introduced the more resilient polymer bank note, which will eventually replace the paper bank note. At present, older paper notes are still in circulation and both types of notes are considered legal tender.

## Banking/ATMs

You will be able to withdraw Canadian dollars from Automatic Teller Machines across Canada, but you should expect to pay a bank fee of $2 to $5, as well as a small percentage for the foreign currency transaction. If your bank is partnered with a Canadian bank, you can save on part of the fee. Bank of America, Barclays Bank in the UK, France, Spain and several African countries, Westpac in Australia, New Zealand, Tonga, Samoa and Fiji, Deutsche Bank, BNP Paribas and affiliate bank brands and Banca Nazionale del Lavoro in Italy are partnered with Scotiabank through the Global ATM Alliance, which means that you will be able to save on some of the usual bank fees, although a percentage charge on foreign currency will still apply. Do remember to inform your bank of your travel plans before leaving home.

## Credit Cards

Credit cards are widely accepted as legal tender across Canada. MasterCard and Visa are commonly accepted by most Canadian shops or businesses, although some travellers have reported problems with Visa in Canada. Walmart recently issued a statement that they will no longer accept Visa at their Canadian outlets, although they still accept MasterCard, American Express and Discover. Canada adapted to chip-and-pin credit card technology several years ago and you should experience no trouble using a card from the UK or European Union. Since financial institutions in Canada no longer accept liability for magnetic strip transactions, American visitors with older magnetic strips may experience difficulty using their credit cards as payment.

## Tourist Tax

At present, Ontario is the only province in Canada that has not yet introduced legislation regarding hotel tax, but a number of cities in the province, such as Toronto, voluntarily collect what is termed as a destination marketing fee of 3 percent. In Vancouver 8 percent provincial tax plus 3 percent municipal tax is levied on hotel accommodation. St Johns in Newfoundland and Labrador levies a 4 percent tax on hotel rooms, while Gros Morne levies 3 percent. In Alberta, a hotel room tax of 5 percent is levied. In Quebec the rate varies, but is usually charged at $2 or $3 or 3 to 3.5 percent per night depending on the location of the accommodation. Winnipeg in Manitoba levies 5 percent, but exempts budget accommodation and hostels. Brandon in Manitoba also levies 5 percent, while Thompson levies $3 per night. Halifax levies 2 percent tax on larger hotels. In Charlottetown in Prince Edward Island, 2 percent tax is levied on tourist accommodation. Bathurst in New Brunswick adds $2 per night for accommodation, while Miramichi, Saint John and Charlotte County levy a municipal tax for tourists of 2 percent. Around Niagara Falls, 3 percent destination marketing fee is levied.

# Claiming Back VAT

In Canada, the tax on purchases and services varies according to province. In Alberta, British Columbia, Manitoba, Nunavut, Northwestern Territories, Saskatchewan and Yukon, a goods and services tax rate (GST) of 5 percent applies. Ontario, Nova Scotia, New Brunswick, Prince Edward Island, Newfoundland and Labrador levy the so-called harmonized sales tax (HST), which combines federal and provincial taxes. The rate of HST is 13 percent in Ontario, New Brunswick, Newfoundland and Labrador, 14 percent in Prince Edward Island and 15 percent in Nova Scotia. Quebec levies 5 percent GST plus 9.975 percent Quebec Sales Tax. In 2007, Canada replaced the existing tax rebates for tourists and non-residents with the Foreign Convention and Tour Incentive Program (FCTIP), which limits rebates to taxes paid for tour packages or conventions. You are eligible if the amount spent exceeds $200 without the tax component and the supplier/tour operator has not yet refunded you through other channels.

## Tipping Policy

In Canada, tipping is common practice and attitudes are generally similar to the USA. It is customary to tip between 10 and 15 percent on your restaurant bill. In most cases, a service charge is not included. In bars, $0.50-$1 per drink is acceptable. If you are having pizza delivered, tip the delivery person. Tip about $2 per bag to hotel porters and tip your taxi driver 10 percent. Hairdressers should also be tipped for good service.

## Connectivity

## Mobile Phones

Canada's mobile phone networks are compatible with networks in the USA, but different from most other networks around the world as it favors CDMA networks, rather than the GSM networks used in most of Europe, Asia and Africa. While this may be technologically convenient for visitors from the USA, there is still the matter of roaming fees, which can be expensive, even for US tourists. Some US service providers do offer special deals for calls from Canada, or the option to limit charges and usage to a pre-set daily rate. Only three Canadian service providers provide close to nationwide coverage. They are Rogers, Telus and Bell. Wind Mobile offers coverage mainly in the urban and semi-urban areas of Canada, but partners with other networks to make up the difference. Additionally, there are a number of regional services, such as Ice Wireless, which covers parts of Inuvik, Yukon and the Northwestern Territories, MTS Mobility in Manitoba, Sasktel Mobility in Saskatchewan, Vidéotron Mobile in Ottawa and Quebec and Eastlink on Canada's Atlantic seaboard.

Canada's mobile industry is geared mainly towards locals, with contracts being preferred over prepaid options and a Canadian credit card being mandatory for the activation of most mobile deals. However, the industry is slowly changing to meet the demands of tourists. Bell is Canada's oldest telephone company, but they have moved with the times. If your main priority is staying connected to the web, your best bet will be their data only sim card, available at about $9.95. You can top-up using a Bell recharge voucher. Rogers is the Canadian carrier that is most compatible with international networks. They offer free sims for the activation with a new phone purchase, but will charge $10 for a replacement sim if you have your own device.

Once you have your sim card, you can choose from various usage plans starting at $30 or choose a pay-per-minute plan with minimum $10 top-ups and the option of data add-ons. Rogers is partnered with Fido and Chatr Mobile.

## Dialing Code

The dialing code for Canada is +1, the same as the United States.

## Emergency numbers

General Emergency: 911

MasterCard: 1 800 307 7309

Visa: 1 800 847 2911

# General Information

## Public Holidays

1 January: New Year's Day

March/April: Good Friday

1 July: Canada Day

First Monday in September: Labor Day

25 December: Christmas Day

Several public holidays are only observed in certain states. The official separation of Nunavut from the North-Western Territories is celebrated in Nunavut on the 9th of July. Quebec observes Easter Monday, National Patriot's Day (on the Monday preceding 25 May) and Jean Baptiste Day, also known as Quebec Day (24 June). Victoria Day falls on the Monday on or before 24 May and it is observed in all states except New Brunswick, Nova Scotia and Prince Edward Island. In the Northwest Territories, 21 June is a Provincial holiday celebrated as National Aboriginal Day. Discovery Day is celebrated in 3 states. In Newfoundland and Labrador, it falls on the Monday closest to 24 June and in Yukon, it is commemorated on the Monday nearest to 17 August. Thanksgiving is celebrated on the second Monday in October in most states, except for New Brunswick, Newfoundland, Nova Scotia and Prince Edward Island. Remembrance Day is observed in most states as a statutory holiday, with the exception of Manitoba, Nova Scotia, Ontario and Quebec. While special events like Mother's Day, Valentine's Day, Father's Day and Halloween are widely observed, they are not holidays. Although not a statutory holiday, Civic Day is observed on the first Monday of August in Alberta, British

Columbia, New Brunswick, Nunavut, Ontario and Saskatchewan.

## Time Zones

Canada is divided into six different time zones. Newfoundland Standard Time is used in the areas of Newfoundland and the south-eastern tip of Labrador. It can be calculated as Greenwich Mean Time/Co-ordinated Universal Time (GMT/UTC) -3 hours and 30 minutes in winter and -2 hours and 30 minutes in summer. Atlantic Standard Time is used in most of Labrador, New Brunswick, Nova Scotia, Prince Edward Island and Quebec. It is calculated as Greenwich Mean Time/Co-ordinated Universal Time (GMT/UTC) -4 hours in winter and -3 hours in summer. Eastern Standard Time (EST) applies in most of Nunavut, Ontario and Quebec and is calculated as Greenwich Mean Time/Co-ordinated Universal Time (GMT/UTC) -5 hours in winter and -4 hours in summer. Central Standard Time (CST) is observed in Manitoba, Saskatchewan and parts of Ontario and can be calculated as Greenwich Mean Time/Co-ordinated Universal Time (GMT/UTC) -6 hours in winter and -5 hours in summer. Mountain Standard Time (MST) is observed in Alberta, the Northwestern Territories, eastern communities in British Columbia, Lloydminster in Saskatchewan and Kugluktuk Cambridge Bay in Nunavut. It is calculated as

Greenwich Mean Time/Co-ordinated Universal Time (GMT/UTC) -7 hours in winter. Pacific Standard Time (PST) applies in Yukon and most of British Columbia and can be calculated as Greenwich Mean Time/Co-ordinated Universal Time (GMT/UTC) -8 hours in winter and -7 hours in summer.

## Daylight Savings Time

Clocks are set forward one hour at 01.00am on the last Sunday of March and set back one hour at 01.00am on the last Sunday of October for Daylight Savings Time. Most of the province of Saskatchewan (except Creighton and Denare Beach) does not observe Daylight Savings Time and neither do Pickle Lake, New Osnaburgh and Atikokan in Ontario, Quebec's North Shore, Southampton Island in Nunavut and Creston in British Columbia.

## School Holidays

In Canada, the academic year runs from mid September to the latter part of June. There is a two week winter break in December and a two week spring break in March. In most provinces, the summer holidays begin on the last Saturday of

June, although Quebec factors in the public holiday on 24 June. Schools begin again on the Tuesday after Labor Day.

# Trading Hours

In Canada, trading hours are regulated at provincial level. In British Columbia, Alberta, and Saskatchewan, as well as Yukon, Northwestern Territories and Nunavut, there are no legislation prohibiting trade at any particular time, but trading hours will usually vary according to the area and the type of business. Common trading hours are from 10am to 6pm from Mondays to Saturdays, with shops also being open from noon to 5pm on Sundays. At larger city malls you can expect late trade on Thursdays, Fridays and Saturdays. In urban areas, there will usually be a pharmacy and convenience store trading 24 hours and some fast food outlets may also trade round the clock. Post Office hours may vary, according to the location of the outlet. In Quebec, shopping hours are set at 9.30am to 5.30pm from Mondays to Wednesdays, 9.30am to 9pm on Thursdays and Fridays, 9.30am to 5pm on Saturdays and 10am to 5pm on Sundays. In Nova Scotia, shops are closed on Remembrance Day, whereas in Manitoba, Quebec, Ontario, New Brunswick and Prince Edward Island, shops are closed on most major public holidays, including Remembrance Day. In those states, Sunday trading is also restricted.

# Driving Policy

Canadians drive on the right side of the road. If you have a valid driver's license in your own country, you should be permitted to drive in Canada, but it may be advised that you apply for an International Driving Permit, which will include a translation of your licence in English and French. The minimum driving age is 16. To drive in Canada, car insurance is compulsory and you will be required to organize a policy that provides adequate cover for your age group and driving experience. If renting a car, check that car insurance is including in your rental agreement. All ten provinces in Canada have legislation restricting the use of mobile phones while driving and requires you to use a hands free kit. Speed limits are given in kilometers. In Canada, the speed limits are set at 110km per hour for multiple lane highways, 80km per hour for 2-lane highways, 60km per hour for urban and suburban roads, between 40 and 50km per hour for residential roads and 30km per hour for school zones.

# Drinking Policy

In Canada, legislation regarding the sale and consumption of alcohol is set at the provincial level. In most provinces, the minimum drinking age is 19, with the exception of Alberta, Manitoba and Quebec, where you can legally drink from 18 years of age. An old law dating back to 1928 prohibits Canadians from transporting alcohol across provincial and national boundaries without permission from the provincial liquor control board. Do bear this in mind, if you are planning to travel through several provinces or territories with your own supply of beer or wine. It is against the law. Of the provinces, Quebec has the most relaxed liquor laws and allows alcohol sales from regular grocery stores.

# Smoking Policy

Smoking legislation is determined at provincial level in Canada. All provinces adopted some form of restriction on smoking in public places and work spaces in the period between 2003 and 2008. In Nunavut, which has the highest percentage of smokers, it is illegal to smoke within 3 metres of a building's entrance. In Toronto, you may not smoke within 9 metres of a building's entrance. In Manitoba, Quebec, Saskatchewan, British Columbia, Nova Scotia, Ontario, New Brunswick,

Newfoundland and Labrador, it is illegal to smoke in a vehicle if minors under the age of 16 are passengers. Alberta also restricts the type of outlets that are allowed to sell cigarettes.

## Electricity

Electricity: 110 volts
Frequency: 60 Hz
Canada uses electricity sockets similar to those found in the USA, with two flat prongs or blades arranged parallel to each other. These are compatible with Type A and Type B plugs. You will also find that appliances from the UK or Europe which were designed to accommodate a higher voltage will not function as effectively in Canada. While a converter or transformer should be able to adjust the voltage, you may still experience some performance degradations with the type of devices that are sensitive to variations in frequency as the Canada uses 60 Hz, instead of the 50 Hz which is common in Europe and the UK.

## Food & Drink

Breakfast in Canada can be a hearty mix of fried bacon, pork sausage, eggs, deep-fried potatoes, toast and pancakes, but continental twists such as French toast and pastries are equally popular, as is cereal. Lunch is generally a light meal such as sandwiches, salads or soup. Traditionally meat is central to the Canadian dinner. Canada also has its own range of tempting sweets and confectionaries. Maple syrup is a staple ingredient of various cookies and pastries. Canadian chocolate bars include the Coffee Crisp, made of coffee flavored wafers smothered in milk chocolate and the Nanaimo Bar, a British Columbian snack with with a rich buttery filling sandwiched between two slices of chocolate. The Beaver's Tail is a lump of deep-fried dough sprinkled with sugar and cinnamon. Poutine is a simple fast food that originated in Quebec and consists of French fries, smothered in cheese and gravy. Sometimes chicken, bacon, sausage, ground beef or other meat is added. Another French-Canadian favorite is Tourtière, or meat pies, usually made of beef, veal or pork. If you have trouble choosing between pizza and pasta, then the Pizza-ghetti is for you. It combines half a pizza with a helping of Spaghetti Bolognaise.

Canadian coffee culture embraces the simplicity of Tim Horton, the country's most popular chain of coffee and doughnut shops, but in recent years, tastes have grown somewhat more sophisticated and cosmopolitan. Bottled glacier water is available across Canada. Coke, Pepsi and Diet Coke are the best selling soft drinks, but for a taste of local flavor, try Jones Soda, which features a range of tastes including green apple, bubblegum, strawberry lime, crushed melon and even peanut butter and jelly. Some of their limited editions include pumpkin pie and poutine flavored soft drinks. Ginger ale is a Canadian invention and another Canadian favorite is clamato juice, a combination of clam chowder and tomato juice, which is combined with vodka to produce the Bloody Caesar, the country's signature cocktail.

Beer is Canada's favorite alcoholic beverage and Budweiser from across the border, its top selling brand. Canadian beer drinkers love to experiment, which accounts for the popularity of craft beers and also the introduction of ice beer amidst fierce rivalry by two of Canada's top beer brewers, Labatt and Molson. Both brands are based in the province of Quebec which has a lively beer brewing tradition and hosts two annual beer festivals, one in Quebec City and one in Montreal. Canadians also produce ice wine, a sweet dessert wine and rye whiskey, of which the award-winning Canadian Club and Crown Royal are its most representative brands.

# Useful Websites

http://wikitravel.org/en/Canada

https://www.attractionscanada.com/

http://www.frontier-canada.co.uk/

http://www.canadianbucketlist.com/

http://transcanadahighway.com/

http://www.tour-guide-canada.com/

http://www.thecanadaguide.com/

Made in the USA
Middletown, DE
15 January 2020

83253296R00053